Other books by Frank Shapiro

Flies (2001)
The Oppositional Teenager (2007)
The Old Man And The Tree (2009)

To Erin—
Who has taught me love
outside the box

Adolescence is a period of rapid changes.
Between the ages of 12 and 17, for example,
a parent ages as much as 20 years.

--Author Unknown

TABLE OF CONTENTS

INTRODUCTION

This program is designed to change your life. That's a rather large boast, but if you have a difficult teenager or are simply having difficulties with your teenager, you would probably welcome a life change.

The truth is, good parenting—especially with tough kids—is far from easy, but the principles of good parenting are actually rather simple. The strategies I present here are timeless, not based on the latest research or trend. This program would have worked two thousand years ago and will work two thousand years in the future. Success for you as a parent hinges on one factor—a willingness on your part to develop a *different way of being*.

The trap most parents fall into is trying to force change on their teenager.

It doesn't work.

You have to change. *You* have to be different. The only way to make your teenager different is for you to be different. There is no other way.

In this book, you will be introduced to seven strategies that will result in a different way of being. What you *do* in particular situations naturally follows. It's not complicated, but as I said earlier, it isn't easy. You will have to make some significant changes in yourself and adopt some new perspectives.

Having difficulties with parenting—and specifically parenting teenagers—is completely understandable. We're expected to be good parents without having any more training in the subject than our own experiences with *our* parents and our intuition.

That's often not enough.

Let's look at this in historical and cultural context. There was a time not long ago when sons and daughters would be managed with intimidation and physical consequences. In other words, respect was established through fear. And this was in many cases effective. If your teenager feared you, he or she would respect you and do what you said.

Today what is acceptable from a parent has changed. In fact, in this day and age if you are physical with your teenager—even harsh verbally—you will not only lose respect, you run the risk of bringing the Department of Family and Child Services into your life.

Parents today have a much tougher task than parents have ever faced before. In many ways, they're expected to do more with less. Technology alone has complicated things. Our kids are exposed to information, commodities, and behaviors much earlier in their lives. They're smarter, savvier, and on the negative side (in many cases) more cunning than in the past.

American culture in the 21st century demands parents raise their skills to a level never previously required.

Now, parenting books and programs are an industry unto themselves. Go to the bookstore or search online and you will find thousands of books on parenting. Each year hundreds of new ones are written.

What does this tell us?

There are a lot of parents out there who need help, and there are plenty of therapists and doctors willing to provide it. You can find just about everything: unconditional love at one extreme, tough love at the other, and numerous approaches in-between. Oddly, none seem to take hold with the public for very long—which leaves room for the next batch the following year. There's a program that's popular right now and advertises regularly on radio and TV. It promises "total transformation" of your defiant child. Of course, it costs over $300 (but the ads don't tell you that!) Further, it comes with a bonus CD that—it says—will turn your child's attitude around in one minute. Makes me wonder why you need the rest of the program!

Actually, I've listened to that program and it has some good ideas in it, as most of them do. And I encourage you to check out different programs and their ideas and techniques.

"Parenting Outside The Box" is a bit different. It is not filled with long-winded explanations or confusing details. It is simple and concise and will give you what you need to do parenting better.

"Parenting Outside The Box" deals in broad themes, not minutia. It will offer you new perspectives and a few key insights that will change the way you feel about parenting and change the way you parent—no more, no less. It's straightforward and no-nonsense, easy to read and understand. It will bring you to areas of thinking you haven't been before.

Now, a little about my credentials. In 2007, I published a book called "The Oppositional Teenager." Its target audience was parents of non-mainstream teens, and it spelled out my understanding of difficult adolescents and strategies for parenting them. What became clear after writing the book and talking to parents was that I had actually written two books in one, and that the parenting strategies included in "The Oppositional Teenager" could apply to all parents of all teenagers.

That's how "Parenting Outside The Box" was born.

I have been a licensed Marriage and Family Therapist in California since 1997. Since 2001 I have worked at North Hills Preparatory School in Los Angeles, a progressive secondary school that serves emotionally-disturbed, AD/HD, learning disabled, and autistic spectrum students. I am not the typical Dean of Students, scaring kids into behaving and dishing out tough punishments when they make mistakes. Instead, it is my role to help students build practical abilities that will serve them in life after high school—self-awareness, self-esteem, direction, discipline, patience, and relationship skills. I work "in the moment," when students are frustrated and upset, when problems are happening. A large part of my job is dealing with parents, who are often confused and overwhelmed by their teenagers. Over the years, I have worked with hundreds of teenagers, and, of course, hundreds of parents.

I use a positive relationship with students as the basis of my approach.

And, quite honestly, *it works*.

Most programs, most approaches and interventions focus on managing and modifying *behavior*. That's fine, but in fact it is only the tip of the iceberg and in a sense actually an illusion. The real challenge is to mold *character* and develop *personality*.

That's a much deeper proposition. It's what I do at school every day and what this program emphasizes.

The benefit is that when this occurs, positive behavior naturally follows.

That's where we'll be going in "Parenting Outside The Box."

So here's what you can look forward to:

After establishing our fundamental goal—a *different way of being*—in the next section, we'll look at the seven strategies that are available to you in reaching this goal. Each strategy is an entity unto itself, but relates to the others and everything ties together. By the time we reach the conclusion, you'll already know what I'm going to say and it will simply reinforce what's been learned. The big picture—which is what "Parenting Outside The Box" emphasizes—will be clear.

You will be on your way to a better relationship with your teenager, increased mutual respect, and fewer behavior problems. Your life—and parenting—will be enjoyable again.

A DIFFERENT WAY OF BEING

"Parenting Outside The Box" does not focus on your teenager.
Its focus is on you, the parent.

In "Parenting Outside The Box", we present principles and strategies that can be applied to any situation, any teenager. But "Parenting Outside The Box" does not focus on your teenager. The focus is on you, the parent. "Parenting Outside The Box" is designed to develop in you a different way of being.

This is about who you *are*. What you *do* in each individual situation follows naturally from this basic position.

You'll see that it becomes easier to know what to do when you tap into how to be. This is a paradigm shift. What's a paradigm shift? It's a different way of seeing and understanding things.

In this program I will be asking you to make a few paradigm shifts, and this is the first: *a different way of being*. Say this to yourself: "A different way of being in myself will change my teenager's attitude and behavior." Say it over and over, memorize it, and eventually live it. This is the key to our enterprise here.

It's probably fair to assume that your teenager has become difficult and what you've done in response has not worked to your satisfaction. That's why you're here with me. Perhaps you've yelled and screamed and threatened and punished, just like most parents do when their power is challenged. In all likelihood, that has made things worse, not better, which leads me to this suggestion:

To be the shock absorber you need to be—rather than the nuclear reactor you probably have been—you will have to change *your way of being*.

This means several things, which this program will teach you:

You will become proactive rather than reactive, assuming a stance of leadership, not authority. There is a difference. You will *invite* your teenager into cooperation instead of exerting arbitrary power or threatening. That's what frustrated, unsuccessful parents do. *You're* going to be different. You're not going to yell, you're not going to scream and become sarcastic, and you're not going to criticize. You're not going to be made crazy by your teenager. You're going to be calm and you're going to be thoughtful. You're going to have a plan in how you approach your child. You're going to know who you are and what you're doing and where you're going. It's a *different way of being*.

You are going to become strong, smart, aware, agile, flexible, and full of stamina.

You will take responsibility for the relationship. You will bring *direction* to your parenting. You will work to *earn* respect rather than demanding it. You will make *your* happiness a priority. You will become *smart* about teenage/parent dynamics. And you will become *skillful* at conversation and negotiation.

You are going to *be* different than you have been, and as a result your teenager is going to become different than he or she has been.

TAKE RESPONSIBILITY

Rather than thinking about what your teenager needs to do,
think about what you can do.

Here's the second paradigm shift I'm asking you to make in "Parenting Outside The Box". No longer is it that "my teenager has a problem" or "my teenager has problems." Now it's *I* have a problem. *I* have problems.

It's you.

It's not him. It's not her.

It's you.

You have a problem.

You may find yourself reacting defensively to this statement. Most parents do. They get excited and raise their voices, saying, "Hey, I'm doing all right! I have a job, I have responsibilities, I take care of things! My kid has the problem! He's the one who doesn't do what he's supposed to! She's the one who's stopped going to school or is smoking marijuana or who's gotten in trouble with the law! He's the one who talks back and has a bad attitude!"

True. You are probably taking care of your business and your teenager is not. But we're not talking here about who's right.

That goes nowhere.

We're talking about how to change a situation.

You have the problem.

The problem is your *relationship* with your teenager. Here we make the fundamental assumption of "Parenting Outside The Box":

The better your relationship is with your teenager, the more mutual respect you'll have and the better he or she will behave within your family, at school, and in the community.

In other words, there is a clear and direct correlation between a positive parent-teen relationship and good behavior generally.

The advantage offered by this perspective is that it puts *you* in the driver's seat, not your teenager. Rather than thinking about what your teenager needs to do, think about what **you** can do. **You are now in control, because you can control your behavior, you can only influence his or her behavior.**

Let's say that again.

You cannot **control** your teenager's behavior, you can only *influence* his or her behavior.

And how do we influence that behavior? That's right. With a *different way of being*.

If you fall into the trap that most parents do—telling your teenager that he or she *has* to change—you will be met with resistance. No one wants to be told they have to change, and especially not a teenager. Most teenagers already feel that there are too many "have-to"s in their life—things that are forced upon them by adults at home and at school. Trying to argue the point by letting them know how much harder you have it and how many more responsibilities you have *will not be constructive*. They'll feel demeaned and they won't learn from it. Trying to impose change on a teenager does not work. He will suck you into a power struggle that you cannot win and in the end you'll end up feeling the way he usually does—powerless.

So here's the trick.

This will require another paradigm shift. Consider this perspective: families are **systems**. Systems are combinations of inter-related objects. In plain speak, what one person does in a family influences the family as a whole as well as each individual member. So, what you do influences what your teenager does. If you make changes in yourself, you influence change in your teenager.

Remember, this is about responsibility—*your responsibility*—and so to change the system, you change yourself. **Ironically, this indirect approach is the most direct route to a better relationship with your teenager.**

Here's an example of what you can say:

"I haven't done a very good job, because, look, you're not doing well in school, you're not happy with me, you're not happy in this family, you're not doing what you're supposed to. I clearly messed up. I apologize for that. I probably should have done a better job. I'm going to start trying to do a better job. I'm not going to force anything on you. I'm going to look at myself in the mirror and I'm going to try to make positive changes. And hopefully those positive changes I make in myself will have a positive impact on you. I can't guarantee it, I can't control what you do, but I'm going to take responsibility for the mess I've made and I'm going to make every effort to fix that mess."

You start the process of change by taking responsibility for the change. You don't get mad, you don't criticize. You become the

agent of change. You are the one who is going to make changes, and your teenager—without even realizing it!—is going to follow your lead.

But remember—they can't follow if you don't lead.

So, parents...*lead!*

PARENT WITH PURPOSE

We're taking the complexity out of parenting
by streamlining our actions toward three specific aims.

Many parents parent unconsciously.

In other words, they parent without carefully reflecting on what they're doing—what premises and assumptions guide them, what strategies work best, even what their goals are. They base their interactions and decision-making on what any particular moment demands, and when stressed they fall back on what was done to them by their parents. Often, this approach is inadequate and parents find themselves arguing with their teenagers and caught up in power struggles that leave everyone unhappy.

Let's jump forward to the bottom-line and consider something many of us don't really think about: what is our goal in parenting?

Oftentimes we get distracted by the day-to-day issues of life and forget this (or never think about it in the first place). We spontaneously move from moment-to-moment, stage-to-stage in our child's life, without any direction organizing our behavior. Many parents assume the whole experience is easier than it is and that things "just work out." However, most parents will tell you that parenting is harder than anything they've ever done, and certainly harder than they expected.

Now, we just used a phrase that I want to repeat and emphasize: "direction organizing our behavior." What we're getting at here is that if we had some basic parenting guidelines to follow, our decision-making—our very lives—would be so much more manageable. We could feel we were actually working toward something and not just fumbling around doing what we can as each situation arises.

"Parenting Outside The Box" has them for you. Your fundamental aims as a parent are to help your child:

1) Be safe

2) Develop independence

3) Feel good about themselves

Let's stop and think about this for a moment. It seems simple, and in fact, it is. We're taking the complexity out of parenting by streamlining our actions toward these three specific aims. In each interaction, in every behavior, and even in each thought you have regarding your teenager, ask yourself these questions: Am I helping my teenager learn self-protection? Am I helping my teenager develop independence? Am I helping my teenager to feel good about him or herself? If it's a "no" to these questions, you probably shouldn't do or say it.

What this does, as I said, is take the confusion out of parenting interactions and direct it.

You're looking as a parent to build independence skills and self-esteem. You're helping your child understand the dangers that exist in this world and to protect him or herself.

You're not looking to vent your frustration or shape your child in your own image or any of the things we do when we're angry or operating unconsciously. By developing your teenager's ability to be safe and independent and to feel good, you're preparing him or her for adulthood.

If everything you do or say is carried out with this in mind, parenting in general will seem less puzzling and you'll feel more decisive about your words and your actions.

You follow your thoughts, not your feelings. This decisiveness will have an impact on your teenager, gaining you respect. Respect then leads to better behavior.

Let's look more closely at the issue of respect next.

EARN RESPECT

Your teenager acts the way he or she does
because your relationship lacks mutual respect.

One of the traps that parents fall into is their belief that they *deserve* respect.

They believe that respect from their children should be automatic. In fact, many parents demand it, and this leads to power struggles that often become ugly. In an effort to assert power that they feel they're entitled to, they go to war with their teenagers. The problem here is that even the victor in war—if there is such a thing—suffers casualties.

If you fight this war, the casualty will be your relationship with your teenager. And without that relationship, you have no chance to influence behavior in a positive way.

Chances are, your relationship with your child is already in peril and here's why. It isn't pleasant to hear, but we need to say it:

Your teenager acts the way he or she does because your relationship lacks mutual respect. Your situation is, at least in part, the product of the lack of respect your teenager has for you, and it's almost certainly due to the lack of respect you show your teenager.

This is another point where most parents react defensively. But I ask you to pause a moment and consider: Would your teenager do the things he does if he cared how you feel? Would he talk back, ignore chores, get into trouble at school or with the law—if he respected you?

No, he wouldn't.

He would attempt to be a better person because he would know

that you are affected by his actions. **And your opinion of him would matter to him.** But because he doesn't respect you, and doesn't feel respected by you, he does what he wants.

In the world of the teenager, respect is a vital issue. Conflicts at school often arise from kids feeling disrespected by peers or teachers or staff. It's really about power--or lack of it. Most teenagers feel powerless. They can't drive, don't work, are without money, and have to live within rules they had no choice in creating.

How do teenagers cope with that lack of real power?

By attempting to assert power wherever they can. The world of respect becomes a major arena for them to play out this dynamic. Teenagers feel they have to be respected first before they will give back respect. In other words, in their world, respect of parents and elders and authority figures is not automatic. It has to be *earned*. That's their power.

Here's what I propose: give it to them. Give them the power they seek.

This may sound completely opposite of what you believe to be "correct" or even "right." I understand. But this isn't about being right. This is about establishing the kind of relationship between you and your child that is positive, valuable, and effective.

So, rather than being "right," consider being "smart." Another paradigm shift. Being smart begins with seeing things as they *are*, not as you think they *should* be.

Once again, you have a choice. You can say, "My teenager has a problem. He doesn't respect me." Or you can say, "I have a problem. My teenager doesn't respect me." Once you make this choice, you can get to work. It is fixable and you're going to fix it. How? That's right: again, with a *different way of being*.

It is likely that if you have a problematic relationship with your teenager your teenager feels disrespected by you and even dis-liked by you. If your relationship is contentious, you have probably said things and acted in ways that have led your teenager to feel this way.

Again, before you defend yourself and tell me about his or her behavior, stop!

How they've acted doesn't matter.

We're talking about *you*.

You cannot be **reactive**. You must be **proactive**. In other words, **you do not act the way you do because of how they act.**

You have to *earn* their respect. The way you do this is 1) you look at the ways that you've *earned* disrespect and you try to correct them, and 2) you start treating them with respect.

There are a number of ways that parents lose the respect of their children and teenagers. Let's list them:

They're unhappy.

They're angry.

They complain.

They appear powerless.

They are critical.

They are negative.

They don't listen.

They're disorganized and sloppy.

They demean and/or negate their children.

They mess up their marriage and break up their family.

They smoke, drink, or take drugs.

Once again, you have to make changes. To change your teenager, you have to change first. Look at that list and acknowledge your shortcomings. Look to make some corrections.

You don't have to be perfect, just better than you have been.

Let's examine some nuts and bolts of your interactions and make a few adjustments.

There are easy ways to let your teenager feel powerful, but the most direct path is by showing respect. Say please and thank you, speak without raising your voice, listen without judgment. I'm going to get into more of this later when we talk about thinking, but right now—don't criticize and don't be judgmental of their culture and what they like. Parents fall into this trap all the time. Whether it's the music their teenagers listen to or their clothing or something else they're interested in or involved in, parents are often negative about it.

You can't be like that with your kid. If you are, they're going to rebel. They're not going to like feeling "less than." And they are going to do everything they can to make your life miserable and make you feel powerless.

Next, show that you genuinely like them. I know, that seems like an obvious thing. But if you demonstrate that you are fed up, discouraged, or disgusted with them, they are going to think you don't like them and they are not going to want to cooperate with you. Think about it. You would not want to cooperate with somebody who clearly didn't like you. Ask them to do things with you. Show interest in their lives and thoughts and feelings—*genuine* interest. If you're fake, they'll see through it.

Remember, you have to *earn* respect. You do so by allowing them to feel some power.

Finally, explain why you're making the decisions you make that affect them. Parents often overlook this element. If you have a curfew, tell them why you have a curfew: "Because that's what I need to feel good about your safety. Problems usually happen after midnight." If you won't buy them something they want, tell them why: "I want you to earn the money to buy that so you'll learn the value of work." Even if they don't agree, if you tell them why and don't fall back on "because I said so," you will do much better. They will feel respected and will respect you because you're parenting with a plan.

So, earn their respect. Look at yourself and make some positive changes. Work hard to respect them. When they respect you back, things fall into place. Your relationship—and their behavior—will improve.

One last thought—they'll also respect you more if you're happy. On to that in the next section.

ROLE-MODEL HAPPINESS

Very often, difficult kids have parents
who haven't figured out how to be happy.

If you ask most parents what their fundamental obligation to their child is you'll get answers like "loving them" or "providing for them financially" or variations on these themes. And they certainly are legitimate answers. Earlier we discussed safety, building self-esteem, and promoting independence as guidelines for parenting interactions. But, since this is "Parenting Outside The Box," I'm going to give you an additional and crucial way of looking at your role as parent—yet another paradigm shift!

To me, your fundamental obligation to your kids is to be happy.

To be happy.

Now think about that for just a minute because it's probably something you haven't heard before in the context of being a more effective parent. Let's look at it a little more closely and see how it makes sense.

In part, your teenager is who he or she is because of who you are. You are the primary role model in your teenager's life, even as they grow up and you lose influence on them to their peers. Who you are has a tremendous influence on your teenager. **Very often, difficult kids have parents who haven't figured out how to be happy.**

The happier you are often correlates to your kid's happiness. So, how do you increase your teenager's level of happiness? Systems thinking, remember? You increase *your own* level of happiness.

Let's say it again: your primary obligation to your kids is to be happy. Happy parents have a much better chance of producing happy kids than unhappy ones do.

You will need to find out how to get happy or get better at expressing your happiness. If that means changing your demeanor, if that means changing your attitude, if that means changing what you do and energizing your life, your job is to be happy.

So once again, this is not your teenager's problem. This is your problem.

Let me say that again. *This is your problem.*

Instead of looking to manipulate your kid's life, what you're doing now is looking within and working on yourself. Because you are the role model and if you role model happiness, there's a greater chance that your kids will, at least to some degree, follow that path.

You're "Parenting Outside The Box". You're leading the way.

You're leading the way with—and to—happiness. Further, you're bringing positive energy into your relationship with your teenager.

Think about what we're saying here. What we're saying is that, typically, your kid is leading the way. **Their unhappiness leads to your unhappiness.**

You have to turn that around.

A teenager should not be leading an adult.

We're talking outside the box. **You have to lead your kid.** And it's leading by example. It's not by preaching to them. It's leading by example. Walking the talk.

Remember: what we're learning here is a different way of being. This is a big jump for a lot of people. Perhaps even scary. "My kid is acting out, my kid is nasty, my kid is *making me miserable.*" It's the passive approach to life and it is not acceptable in this program. You have to turn this around in your mind. You're *allowing* yourself to be made miserable. You have to stop that. No matter what your teenager sends your way, you stay on track.

Now, again, you may be saying, "What is this? I thought I was going to learn how to fix my teenager. I didn't plan on having to fix myself!"

Exactly.

Once again, it's all about *you.*

Your child learns from you—indirectly, as with much of this program—how to be happy. But here's the catch: do you know what it takes to be happy? *Most of us don't.* If you ask people, well, what do you want from life, 90 percent of them will say in a superficial and offhand way, "I want to be happy." But if you ask those people what it takes to be happy, they'll be hard-pressed to provide a satisfactory answer. They're bound to reply with fantasies like "I want to win the lottery" or "I want to travel" or "I want to quit my job."

Important as it is to people, happiness is not something that is taught in school.

Basic psychology isn't even required in our educational system. To graduate high school your child is going to need a lot of English and Math and Science and History, but they'll never learn the basics of being happy. Most of us are never taught this, and in fact never learn it on our own. And that's sad because there are scholars and psychologists who have studied and experimented and charted this out, but it's remained a secret.

In fact, being happy comes from having activities that you can get lost in. Doing work that you enjoy. Developing mastery in a field or endeavor. Valuing your existence. Appreciating nature and art and aesthetics. Having people you can talk to and share your experiences with. Feeling strong and fit and flexible. Having a measure of control over what happens to you and the ones you love.

It's a perspective you can actually choose and create.

Life doesn't just happen to you. **It is what you make of it.**

Therefore, *you* can start by initiating a campaign of personal self-improvement.

Bear with me for a moment because I know we're way out of the box here. Look at your own life (not your teenager's) and find a few areas where you can make changes and improvements, and start working. Whether it's beginning an exercise program or a diet, beginning personal psychotherapy, enrolling in a class, taking up a new hobby, even just noticing and focusing on the good in life and not the bad—make some positive changes in yourself and get going now.

The result of this is that you strengthen yourself and take some of your focus off your teenager. You become stronger and tougher and happier—certainly less consumed by your teenager's actions. Your teenager loses the power that his or her bad behavior is creating in yours and your family's life *because you're too busy to get bogged down with that!* Then, by putting out that good vibe your own life is generating, whatever gets thrown at you—whether it's problems or bad attitudes or dubious behavior—you can absorb it and go about your merry way and not be overwhelmed.

Let's quickly be specific about three things you can do to improve your level of happiness and as a result your role-modeling for your teenager.

1) *Pay attention to your physical well-being.*

Physically fit people generally are stronger, happier people. If you're sedentary and overweight (most Americans are), if you smoke, use drugs, or drink too much, you have to think about making some changes. It's a cliche, but a healthy diet and regular exercise is a fundamental element of personal well-being.

2) *Make having a good attitude a priority.*

If you believe that people are idiots, that's what your kids learn. If your relationships are problematic, your child learns that relationships are problematic. If you get angry easily, your children learn that life makes you angry. Or that life is hard. Or if you hate your job, you role-model that work is a lousy part of being an adult.

You certainly can't blame them then if they don't want to work—don't want to grow up, period!

A good attitude is contagious—just as a bad attitude is.

3) *Examine your use of free time.*

If you come home from work and you drop down on the couch with a beer, spending the night watching TV, that's what your kids' see and that's what your kids are going to think it means to be an adult and a parent. Especially if this is the only time they see you not being mean, angry, or unhappy.

But if you come home and you're repairing a classic car, or you're knitting an afghan, or you're playing a musical instrument, or painting pictures, or whatever it is that you may do, your kid sees that also. They see that there are joys in activities and productivity, and that's important because a key aspect of teenage development is finding a positive identity. If your teenager doesn't find a positive identity and develop the elements that create one, he or she will fill that void with negative activities and ultimately a negative identity.

And you will suffer because of it.

So, the bottom line, again: get happy and express your happiness. Pay attention to your health, pay attention to your attitude, pay attention to your use of free time.

Set a positive example.

The unintended by-product of all this is that you will have improved yourself, no matter what your teenager ultimately chooses to do. You will be a happier person, better equipped to take on the challenges of life, parent-related or otherwise.

UNDERSTAND PSYCHODYNAMICS

You have to understand teenage development, your own reactions, and relationship dynamics to successfully parent your teenager.

Hidden beneath the surface of your everyday relations with your teenager are a number of forces that influence how you behave and how your teenager behaves. What happens to a lot of parents is they don't understand these forces and, because of that, they become confused and lose their "parenting balance."

And because they don't have a way of understanding a particular situation—or their predicament generally—they work off their emotional reactions.

And their emotions are erratic, and then their parenting is erratic.

And then their teenagers are erratic.

And then parents wonder why everything is erratic!

And when we look at it like that, it makes sense, doesn't it?

As you embark on this journey to rework your relationship with your teenager—and your relationship with yourself as a parent, to develop a *different way of being*—it is next important that you get smarter.

Understanding some basic parent-teen psychodynamics is essential to establishing a different way of being. You have to understand aspects of parent psychology, teenage development, and relationship dynamics to optimally parent your teenager.

Once again, we put the spotlight on **you**, not your teenager. This is "Parenting Outside The Box," and as we said earlier, you and your teenager are part of a system where each part has an influence on the other. If you can lift up your level of knowledge and the quality of your interactions, you lift the entire relationship—no matter what your teenager does.

Let's first look more closely at the very nature of parenting. This is often overlooked by teen "experts" because they focus on the teenager and not on the parent. This misses the whole area of *parent psychodynamics*. This is a crucial realm where "Parenting Outside The Box" is decidedly *outside the box*!

One thing to acknowledge right away is the **meaning** our kids have in our lives. Two aspects are important: one, they are a reflection of us; and two, they are our representatives out in the world.

If you sit with that for a moment and really consider it, you take yourself a step forward. Because of the significant meaning our kids have in our lives it is very hard for us to be objective and emotionally-detached when it would behoove us to be. Their behavior—their very being—has a huge impact on **our** psychology.

What happens when you have a child is that child (and later, teenager) becomes an extension of you. In essence, they're almost still connected by that umbilical cord, but now it's invisible and it's psychological.

They're *you*. They look like you, they talk like you, they walk like you.

They're a little representation of you out in the world. And so you're very invested in that little you out there and in what happens to the little you out there. You may even be controlling about that little you out there. It is easy to become *over-invested* in our kids and forget that they're really individuals—separate people on their own in the world who have to figure out much of it by themselves!

Not realizing this—or not accepting it—many parents bring added pressure to bear on their kids, pressure to be *who they want them to be, sometimes even who they **need** them to be.*

You have to stop bringing pressure to bear on your kid because your kid already has enough pressure.

Whether you understand it or not, whether you think he or she does or not, they do. It's the nature of being a teenager. Pressure is actually an aspect of the human condition, no matter what a person's age. Just like you feel the pressure to make a living and the pressure to take care of your family, your teenager feels pressure.

For a teenager, it's the pressure to understand who he is. To live up to expectations. Pressure to figure out who his true friends are. What to invest his energy into. Whether she can make it on her own. What it means to be independent. *Whether people that don't have to love her will love her.* And whether he or she is going to be able navigate all of this.

The mistake many parents make is not acknowledging and understanding the pressure that their teenagers feel. We spoke of this earlier. They compare it to the pressure they have to make a living and take care of their family and minimize it, even dismiss it. Teenagers often feel that their parents don't understand them and disapprove of their every move.

The bottom-line is your teenager doesn't need *more pressure* from you.

As parents, if we understand it's the nature of parenting to be over-invested, we can start practicing to disinvest ourselves. Separate emotionally from our kids. Accept that they're separate people— that *we're* separate people. Treat them as individuals, not as an extension of ourselves. And when you do that, and you can get good with it, then you take much of the negative intensity out of your relationship with your kid.

You actually relieve some of that pressure rather than adding to it, as most parents do.

You must allow your teenager to become who they will become, not who you want or need them to become.

Next, let's focus in on understanding teenage development. It is natural and normal for your teenager to press for independence. That's **normal** development—to separate from their family of origin, develop an identity, and establish significant relationships outside the home.

Teenagers often look grown up, but they are still, on some level, little kids who are very dependent on you. They know it and they hate it—and it's unconscious. Given that, it's very natural for your kid to be rebellious toward you, to challenge your attitudes and opinions, all that stuff. Partly it's to feel more independent, partly it's to rebel against their unconscious dependence. Rather than getting mad at them, you have to encourage that and accept it. If you do, you are far ahead of the game. You will take a huge step closer to *a different way of being* and "Parenting Outside The Box."

Your strategy here is to help them develop **true** independence.

Teenagers often inaccurately equate the growing freedom they have with independence. They naively think it's the same thing. Without really thinking about it, you might as well. But freedom is not independence. **Independence is freedom *combined* with responsibility.**

Let's go over that again, because it's important. What your teenager will do is equate freedom with independence. In an effort to feel powerful and not dependent on you, they will flex their "freedom muscles" and lure you into power struggles. If you're not careful, this dynamic can make a mess of your relationship.

The trick here is to educate your teenager on the difference between freedom and independence in a respectful way. You say something like, "I'll offer you the freedom you desire, but it comes with responsibility. Are you willing to take the responsibility as well as the freedom? If you are, great. Then you're developing independence and I'm all for that. If not, it's not ok with me. That's little kid stuff to want freedom without responsibility."

Most teenagers will accept the challenge. And then rather than losing yourself in endless power struggles that disrupt your family, you enhance their development toward independence, which is good for both of you. Everyone wins.

Try it.

Finally, there's a particular relationship dynamic that must be discussed if we are to truly achieve a *different way of being*. I call this dynamic "sharing it out." But it's not the good kind of sharing!

Sharing it out happens when you feel something and you hold it in, as life often requires us to do. For instance, you're angry about something. And what happens is that when you come in contact with me—me who has nothing to do with the situation that got you mad—you're going to send some of that anger my way. Whether you act angrily toward me or simply carry an attitude, you're going to give me some of that.

It's all unconscious. People have no idea in the moment that they're doing it.

Those feelings want to escape. They want to escape and for that to happen they have to find another person. It's a dysfunctional way of getting relief when we don't get relief by talking it out.

Your kid is not often going to tell you something made him "sad" or "frightened" or "angry." They're going to act something out to make those feelings escape. They'll share out that feeling. When they're angry, they're going to try to make you angry. When they're frightened, they'll try to make you frightened. When they're sad, they're going to try to make you sad. Or they'll jumble them up. They'll be sad, and they'll try to make you angry. Or they'll be angry and try to frighten you. They'll draw a feeling out of you.

Again, they do this because they're trying to relieve themselves in a dysfunctional way. And, remember, this is all *unconscious*. When human beings "share it out," they have no idea that they're doing so!

And if you don't know this, if you're not aware of what goes on, you will fall into the trap of taking on your teenager's feelings. And if you fall into that trap, you will damage your relationship and lose the respect that is your link to their behavior. Remember, if they respect you, their behavior will improve.

And be further forewarned. Teenagers aren't the only ones who "share it out." Adults do it too, all the time. I do it, you do it. Be aware of this! Catch yourself in the act before it goes too far. If you come home from work and you're angry, you might foist this anger onto your teenager to relieve yourself. If you do, you're not only damaging your relationship and losing respect, you're teaching your teenager that it's ok to do this. You're parenting unconsciously. And that's not what we do in "Parenting Outside The Box."

So remember what we've covered here because it's complex and important.

First, understand yourself and the nature of parenting. You have likely become unconsciously psychologically merged with your child. Disinvest from your teenager! Understand their need to figure out who they're going to be without pressure from you.

Second, accept that it's normal development for your teenager to want to separate and gain independence. Accept that and—as we'll see in the next chapter—even encourage it. But teach them the distinction between freedom and independence.

Third, understand that your teenager will try to share out his or her feelings in order to gain relief from the pressure that they're feeling and they'll bait you into reacting. If you can resist reacting negatively and be the shock absorber we discussed way back in the Introduction (remember, as opposed to a nuclear reactor?) you'll avoid destructive power struggles and go far toward developing the relationship you need to improve their behavior.

And with that, watch yourself. Don't share out *your* feelings uncon-sciously. Or if you do (because at some point we all do) apolo-gize! This will take your relationship a step further and once again earn you respect.

ENCOURAGE THINKING

One of the ways you adopt a *different way of being*
is to become a great conversationalist with your teenager.

When children are young, they experience the world almost entirely through their feelings. They feel something and they act on it. They don't think with sophistication. Gradually though the years more complex cognitive processes develop. As adults, our thinking selves should manage our lives. For instance, we want to buy something because we know it will make us happy, but we resist because we cannot afford it or because that money can be better spent elsewhere.

As teenagers, our kids often look like they're all grown up, but they're really not yet. They're still operating primarily off of their feelings and not off of their thoughts. **Another of your jobs as a parent, therefore, is to encourage thoughtfulness.**

Now, how do you do that?

You do that through the art of conversation, and one of the ways you adopt a *different way of being* is you become a great conversationalist with your teenager.

What's the key to being a great conversationalist?

Talk *with* them. Not *to* them, not *at* them—*with* them.

Instead of telling them how things are, ask them what they think about things. Ask a lot of questions, demonstrate interest, don't show judgment, don't criticize, and don't interrupt. Make them feel good about talking to you. If they feel good about talking to you, they'll talk to you more.

Here's a brief example of what I'm getting at, from my book "The Oppositional Teenager."

First, an example of a typical bad exchange:

"I told the idiot teacher to shut up."

"You what?! What kind of a stupid thing was that to do?"

"He is an idiot. Everyone thinks so."

"If everyone thought you should jump off a bridge, would you do it? What you said was ridiculous."

"The class laughed when I said it."

"They're morons."

Now, an alternative approach:

"I told the teacher to shut up."

"Wow, what was your thinking there?"

"He's an idiot. Everyone thinks so."

"How come everyone is so down on this guy? Teaching seems to me like a tough job."

"The class laughed when I said it."

"I wonder how the teacher felt after that."

Be clever about asking questions. "Why did that happen? Oh. And what did you think? Wow...and then what happened?" All of that.

The more they talk, the more they think. The more they think, the more complex their minds become. The more complex their minds become, the more they're able to deal with situations in a sophisticated way. They have a wider repertoire of responses they can apply to their lives. They're not just acting on their feelings. They understand things a little bit better.

Further, talking together means you're spending time together and building your relationship, and by asking questions and listening you show your teenager respect. By showing them respect, you gain respect. The more respect you have from your teenager, the better your relationship will be and the better your relationship is, the better they will behave generally. It becomes a positive, self-perpetuating process!

Bear in mind, again, that you must carry on your conversations without judgment.

Now, stop and focus your attention for a moment—for several moments, because this is crucially important. We spoke of it earlier and it bears repeating. You cannot be judgmental. You probably are—without even realizing it—and it's damaging your relationship with your teenager. The more you've done it the harder it is to undo it, but it can be undone. You have to understand what judgmental is and get rid of it.

Judgmental is negative commentary on your teenager's existence. It's making him or her feel "less than." They already feel that way (due to their lack of *real* power), and the last thing they need is you doing it. It's the last thing you need as well because it damages your relationship, loses you respect, and costs you the ability to influence them in a positive way.

There is an art to being a good conversationalist. Again, get good at asking questions and actually listening to the answers. Then, don't criticize or make negative comments. None. Ask more questions.

And don't interrupt! That's an act of disrespect.

Give your teenager the experience of sharing his or her experience without interruption or judgment. It's empowering to your teenager and, as we've said, it strengthens your relationship. Your teenager gets to not only feel safe with you, but it expands his freedom to talk—to think out loud—with you there to stimulate his mind. The more he thinks, the smarter he gets, and the smarter he gets the better he gets at dealing with life. And that's good for everyone.

Ask questions. Stimulate thinking. Don't judge. Don't criticize. Allow him or her to feel safe.

Do that and everyone benefits.

MANAGE YOUR LEVERAGE

Parents who struggle with their teens
are often not good negotiators.

The final way in which you can improve your parenting—and with that your relationship with your teenager, your mutual respect, and their behavior—is to become an better negotiator. Parents who struggle with their teens are often not good negotiators. They either give their leverage away or never use it to their advantage.

So, let's look at how you can negotiate with your teenager and in so doing improve your relationship and their behavior.

A common trap parents fall into is they do x-y-and-z for their kids, they give, give, give, give, give, and they have kids that don't appreciate the giving and they want more and more and more. Then the parents get resentful and mad and say "I give, give, give and you don't appreciate it."

It's especially difficult in our culture where there are a seemingly endless number of gadgets and toys that kids want. Parents tell me, "Well, you know what, I give my kid a cell phone, I give my kid a computer, I give my kid an iPod, I give my kid all these things and they should appreciate it and respect me, and they don't. My kid has a problem."

We're "Parenting Outside The Box," though.

It's not our kid's problem.

Whose problem is it?

That's right, it's *our* problem. It's *your* problem.

You have a problem because you gave, gave, gave and got nothing back or not enough.

You can't give away your leverage, then complain that you don't have leverage. You'll become resentful and angry toward your kid. You may be there already. And if you're resentful and angry, you're not going to have a good relationship, and if you don't have a good relationship you've lost respect and you have no chance of influencing their behavior.

Now some parents think, well, that's my job as a parent to give, give, give. And to an extent, that's true. You brought your child into the world and you are obligated to take care of him or her as best you can. But you've got to be able to read your situation to be effective. Some people have easy kids. They appreciate what they get and show their parents respect. But my guess is if you have easy, compliant, happy kids, you're not here with me.

Again, the mistake that most struggling parents make is giving their kids something for nothing. *And after years of giving your kid something for nothing, your kid has learned that it's ok for them to get something for nothing. They come to expect that. And when they expect it, you have a huge problem.*

If your kid is either selfish by nature or has learned from you to expect something for nothing, you don't have their respect. You have become a need-fulfilling object rather than a human being. But there is hope. It's a very simple process called **give and take**.

What give and take means is **not** that you give and they take. That's what a lot of teenagers think!

Let me say that again: **Give and take *does not mean* that you give and they take!**

It is the nature of being a teenager to be very self-absorbed and sometimes selfish. They often think they are the center of the universe, not just another one of the billion stars up there. They think everything revolves around them like the planets revolve around the sun.

What I'm suggesting in give and take is that you don't give your kids anything without expecting something back. And you make this crystal clear.

Let's be specific about something for a moment to sharpen the point. Take the cell phone, for example. Cell phones are very important to teenagers. So let's say you get your kid a cell phone with x amount of text messages and minutes and whatnot. You must be very explicit at the beginning about what's expected. "This is how many minutes you have. This is how many text messages you have. If you exceed it, I'm not going to get mad, but your phone is going to get turned off."

You lay this out in advance. Have them agree to the conditions. **In a best-case scenario, have them help develop the conditions.** Then if they mess up, you can tell them: "Hey, you helped set up this contract."

Don't make the mistake many parents make and expect that their teenagers are going to have the discipline and respect to honor you and follow appropriately. What they will do in many cases is be undisciplined and uncaring and follow their pleasure instinct and do whatever they want.

They'll exceed their minutes, they'll exceed their texts, and you're going to get a giant bill.

I've seen this in so many cases. Believe me. And the parent ends up feeling mistreated and powerless. And with some parents this happens month after month after month.

Well, if that's the case, you're being a weakling and you're not parenting positively. So the conditions have to be made explicit. In order to have your cell phone and have me pay for it, this is what I expect in return.

Now of course, you'll be reasonable, and maybe it's chores, maybe it's simply just not exceeding what's allowed in the phone plan. Maybe it's other things. Maybe it's that there's not going to be any disrespectful language in the house. So it could be chores, could be respect, but be very explicit about these things. If you're not explicit, your kid will be a little lawyer and give you the "Oh, you never said anything about that."

So make the implicit explicit. Spell things out in advance. Work with your teenager in setting up agreements. Don't give your kid anything for nothing. Leave yourself the ability to take away whatever it is if need be. This is give and take. I will give you this, I expect this back.

What you're teaching your teenager is the art of business.

In business you get something and you give something. And if an agreement or contract is not followed through on, there are natural consequences. This is an important life lesson that we all need to learn, and if you're not teaching this you're shortchanging your child's potential for independence. That's detrimental to him or her, and it's detrimental to you.

Negotiate in good faith, expect good faith in return, and if you get it point that out to them. Give them the positive attention. But if your good faith is not returned, follow-through on the agreement and let them feel a little pain of loss. They'll survive, they'll learn, and you will gain respect.

CONCLUSION

So here we've arrived at the conclusion of "Parenting Outside The Box".

It hasn't been a long journey, but we *have* covered some significant territory. We've looked at things a little differently than most books and programs do. We've steered away from behavior management and looked instead at character and personality development—for both our teenagers *and* ourselves. The bottom line premise we've established is that in order to improve your life with your teenager, you're going to have to be the agent of change.

Let's review and reinforce what we've learned.

We're operating from a **systems** premise. The systems premise posits that change in one part of the system changes the system. We accept that directly trying to force change on a teenager, looking him in the eye, pointing at him and demanding "You have to change" doesn't work. The reality is that the way you change your teenager is *indirectly* and it comes from changing yourself.

How do you change yourself?

You adopt a *different way of being*.

There are seven strategies you utilize to develop this different way of being.

Number one, **you take responsibility for the problem—the relationship with your teenager**—and you take responsibility for fixing it. You say, "I have a problem. I will make changes in myself in order to change this system and address the problem."

Number two, you operate with a sense of direction and **parent with purpose**. You help your children learn how to keep themselves safe, you work to build their self-esteem, and you encourage their independence. In so doing, you prepare them for adulthood.

Number three, you **earn their respect**. You earn their respect by getting your life in order and respecting them. You respect them by listening to them and not criticizing them. You act in a polite manner by saying "please" and "thank you" to them—and not sarcastically. That doesn't mean indulging them, but it does mean treating them as you would treat a colleague at work or even a stranger you don't know, because in many cases parents treat that colleague or stranger better than their own kid. Why? Because that colleague or stranger hasn't made your life difficult. Your kid has. But you're now going to start fresh with a new attitude and approach. You're going to earn respect by giving respect. You don't criticize, you listen without interruption or judgment, you explain why you make the decisions you make that affect them

Number four, you **role model happiness**. You figure out what it takes for you to be happy, what it takes to express your happiness, and you bring that into your household and into your relationship with your teenager. If you're happy, there's a better chance that your teenager will be happy. Independent of how it affects your teen, getting happy is better for you.

Next, you get smart. You **understand the psychodynamics** that go on in parent-teen relationships. You accept that there's a natural tendency for parents to become over-invested in their kids and want to live their lives for them. Over-invested parents bring additional pressure into their relationships with their teenagers and destroy any chance of building mutual respect, which is the key to influencing behavior. You acknowledge that your teenager is going to rebel against you in various ways in an effort to gain independence, and you absorb their challenges to your authority. You're going to teach them the difference between freedom and independence and in so doing encourage and build healthy independence, which is positive for both of you. Finally, you're going to understand the concept of "sharing out" feelings and not let that dynamic poison your relationship.

Lastly, two things—numbers six and seven—**you become a great conversationalist and you become a great negotiator.**

In conversation, your main goal is to **encourage their thinking,** so you're asking a lot of questions, you're prompting them to talk. The more they talk, the more they express themselves, the better they're able to think and the better they're able to think, the better they're able to respond to all the different kinds of situations that get thrown at them.

Finally, you become more expert at **managing your leverage.** And that comes from being a good negotiator. You don't give something for nothing if your kid's not going to appreciate it. Everything is give and take, which doesn't mean you give and they take. Work with your kid in setting up agreements. It's business, and don't get mad when they mess up. Just follow-through on the agreement you've made together. Don't react out of your feelings. Let your thoughts guide you.

Putting all of this into play—or even just some of it—creates in you *a different way of being.* That different way of being is transmitted to your teenager. The result is less conflict, increased respect, and a better relationship, which then leads to better behavior.

It's all pretty simple, but not easy.

You can do it!

And when you've got all of this, when these strategies come naturally, you're there.

You're "Parenting Outside The Box"!

ACKNOWLEDGEMENTS

Many, many people have contributed to my thinking and the writing and production of this book, and I can only thank some of them. Pete and Rose Shapiro, Jay Shapiro and Jill Archer make up my family of origin. I not only love them, I appreciate them as *parents* and have learned from them. Their support has always been there. Patty, Sean, and Casey Shapiro have tolerated my egocentricity for years. My life with them has made me a better parent—and a better person. Their reading of my work and my discussions and experiences with them have been invaluable.

Ed Queair has been my longtime editor. Erin Papenbrook has listened and read and listened and listened some more. I have benefitted greatly from her love and support.

Working at North Hills Preparatory School has been a godsend for my development. I thank Claire Bowman and Elin Bradley for enabling me to express my ideas and put them into practice, no matter how far "outside the box" they are.

ABOUT THE AUTHOR

Frank Shapiro is a licensed Marriage and Family Therapist practicing in Los Angeles, California. In addition to serving as Dean of Students at North Hills Preparatory, a progressive non-public school, he maintains a private practice focusing on personal and relationship development. ""Parenting Outside The Box"" is his fourth published book.

LaVergne, TN USA
30 May 2010
184491LV00006B/56/P